Contents

D1329244

COVER TO COVER

BIBLE **STUDY**

7 SESSIONS FOR SMALL GROUP
AND PERSONAL USE

Zechariah

SEEING GOD'S BIGGER PICTURE

CWR

Steve Bishop

Published 2020 by CWR, Waverley Abbey House, Waverley Lane, Farnham, Surrey GU9 8EP, UK. CWR is a Registered Charity – Number 294387 and a Limited Company registered in England – Registration Number 1990308.

The right of Steve Bishop to be identified as the author of this work has been asserted by him in accordance with the Copyright, Designs and Patents Act 1988 sections 77 and 78.

For a list of National Distributors, visit cwr.org.uk/distributors

Scripture references are taken from the Holy Bible: New International Version® Anglicised, NIV® Copyright © 1979, 1984, 2011 by Biblica, Inc ® Used by permission, All rights reserved worldwide.

Concept development, editing, design and production by CWR.

Every effort has been made to ensure that this book contains the correct permissions and references, but if anything has been inadvertently overlooked the Publisher will be pleased to make the necessary arrangements at the first opportunity. Please contact the Publisher directly.

Cover image: AdobeStock

Printed in the UK by Linney

ISBN: 978-1-78951-263-2

Introduction

It was a winter afternoon on the English south coast. A very familiar part of the world for me, although my visits from London were normally undertaken in the summer. Now, however, the shoreline was very different. This section of the coast was in the comparatively sheltered calm of a bay, but I was nevertheless experiencing the full-on sights and sounds of the elements in a noticeably turbulent form! The waves were crashing against the promenade and the fierce wind was exerting a powerful force that made walking difficult. To this was added the incessant sea spray that beat against exposed skin and caused the air to be full of the scent and taste of salt water. The overall effect was to considerably enliven and energise my physical senses.

Capturing that scene on my camera or smartphone might later bring back vivid memories but it wouldn't totally capture what was actually experienced. There is an increasing trend for life to be lived through a prism of technology. Scenes and events are captured on video, or streamed, and transmitted for us to 'like' or 'comment' upon. Although it has its value, watching videos does not enable us to appreciate and embrace the full perspective of what is taking place; our expectations of what it would be like to be present in certain moments or environments are limited.

Expectations

Similarly, our perspective of God is not all that it could be. There are many factors that can restrict our ability to see God's bigger picture. One of these is what we 'see' through the prism of our expectations.

Expectations were a big factor in the lives of God's people in the Old Testament. Sadly, these never seemed to be very

high. When they were miraculously freed from Egyptian slavery by God through Moses, their restricted outlook meant that they could only see desert – with little food or water. Their low expectation led them to reminisce about the provision of 'pots of meat' they'd previously had in Egypt (Exod. 16:3). When they eventually reached the brink of the Promised Land, their 'prism' meant that they could only see giants and subsequent defeat (Deut. 1:26–28). A new generation of Israelites under the leadership of Joshua did secure this land, but the influence of surrounding nations lowered their expectation of the reality of God's presence and power. The people rejected God's rule and demanded that a king rule over them instead (1 Sam. 8:4–9). Under King David, Israel achieved great material and spiritual heights, but after the reign of King Solomon (David's son), the nation fragmented into two kingdoms. The larger of these (Israel) persistently made decisions based on human perspective and blind expectations, such as worshipping idols. It resulted in God's judgment by means of invasion and annihilation by the Assyrian Empire in 722 BC.

Self-interest
The remainder of God's people, the nation of Judah, failed to learn from their compatriots. Their continued refusal to heed God's warnings were based on low expectations coupled with high self-interest. It resulted in God's discipline, allowing them to be overrun by the Babylonian Empire in 586 BC. Despite being forced into exile, the Israelites maintained their separate identity and eventually God enabled them, under the newly emerged Persian Empire, to return home. However, it is estimated that only around fifty thousand Israelites actually took up this offer. Again, expectations were a factor. Most of the Israelites chose to stay put, knowing that the journey home would involve travelling a long distance through difficult and

hostile terrain. On top of that, their homeland would be very different from what their forebears had known: the city of Jerusalem was now in ruins, the Temple destroyed and the area surrounded by belligerent people groups.

Galvanised

For the Israelites who did choose to return to Judah, there were significant obstacles to re-establishing God-centred lives. Although work commenced on constructing another temple in Jerusalem in 536 BC, it barely got beyond the foundations being laid. Surrounding people groups and enemies of Israel brought pressure to bear so that construction was halted (Ezra 4:4–21). God's people decided to lower their expectations and focus on just rebuilding their own homes. However, God Himself had different ideas. Haggai was the first of two prophets whom God used to galvanise and motivate His people. Through Haggai God told His people, 'Because of my house, which remains a ruin, while each of you is busy with your own house… I called for a drought on the fields' (Hag. 1:9,11). However, He also encouraged them by saying, 'The glory of this present house [temple] will be greater than the glory of the former house' (Hag. 2:9).

Over a period of around four months, Haggai brought God's 'carrot and stick' methodology to encourage action with regard to rebuilding the Temple and following His ways. Expectations were being raised. But they were to be raised considerably higher by Haggai's fellow prophet, Zechariah. He was to describe God's perspective and intervention in a clearly full-on way.

The rebuilding of the Temple highlights the issue of expectations with regard to God whose plans and ways of working are often outside our experience. The apostle Paul reminds us: 'Now to him who is able to do immeasurably

more than all we ask or imagine' (Eph. 3:20). Zechariah's prophecy aimed at helping God's people – including us – see His bigger picture for this world.

Are you ready for God to expand your expectations and perspective?

WEEK ONE

Back to basics

Opening Icebreaker

Gather a selection of instruction sheets as provided with self-assembly furniture or model construction kits, and identify what is common about the instructions, especially with regard to the initial steps.

Bible Readings

- Zechariah 1:1–6
- Ezra 5:1–2
- Nehemiah 12:1–4
- 2 Chronicles 7:12–21
- Luke 3:7–14
- Revelation 3:14–22

Opening Our Eyes

'Riding a bicycle is about getting back to basics. It's good for the waistline and it's good for the wallet' (Phil Keoghan, New Zealand and US TV personality). Advocating an environmentally friendly and economically viable means of getting around is not the only area in which 'back to basics' is a buzz phrase. It often appears in the sporting world, particularly if a team has suffered a series of defeats. In such circumstances, the coach is likely to utter the mantra about players needing to get 'back to basics'.

The Old Testament describes God's people as constantly going through bad spells – not in a sporting context but in spiritual terms. However, the need to get 'back to basics' was the same. This was the directive when they returned to their homeland after God had miraculously intervened to free them from enforced exile. But once in Judah, and particularly in Jerusalem, they were not in a good place spiritually – as evidenced by their failure to press on with reconstructing the Temple. We might wonder why this was a priority for God, but rebuilding the Temple would be a positive sign that His people were keen to follow His ways.

As a consequence of the Israelites' failure to begin reconstruction, God sent two prophets, Haggai and Zechariah (Ezra 5:1–2). Haggai was the first onto the scene: 'In the second year of King Darius, on the first day of the sixth month' (Hag. 1:1). Zechariah followed 'In the eighth month of the second year of Darius' (Zech. 1:1). Darius reigned from 522–486 BC, meaning that it was 520 BC when both these prophets appeared.

Initial message
Introduced as the 'son of Berekiah, the son of Iddo' (Zech. 1:1), the reference to Iddo shows Zechariah to have been born into

a priestly family (see Neh. 12:1–4). His initial message was pointed and stated the obvious: 'The LORD was very angry with your ancestors' (Zech. 1:2). The devastation arising from the Babylonian invasion culminating in the destruction of Jerusalem in 586 BC evidenced God's anger. Zechariah's hearers not only needed reminding about His anger but urgently needed to respond themselves. The prophet's own name was poignant in this respect: Zechariah, in Hebrew, means 'The LORD remembers'.

God's people were being urged to '"Return to me," declares the LORD Almighty' (v3), reinforced with references to the past and rhetorical questions: 'they would not listen or pay attention to me, declares the LORD. Where are your ancestors now? And the prophets, do they live for ever?' (vv4–5).

Anger
God had not changed His mind or lowered His standards. The Jewish people needed to get 'back to basics'. God's message reiterated through Zechariah was clear: 'Turn from your evil ways and your evil practices' (v4). This command had previously fallen on deaf ears, hence the terrible consequences of the past as foretold by earlier prophets.

Essential step
God's message via Zechariah and Haggai produced a positive spiritual response from His people by way of repentance. They acknowledged their evil inclinations and turned back to God – an essential step that they needed to take themselves. Like underachieving athletes, they had to respond personally – a coach could not do it on their behalf. So they rebuilt the Temple as urged by Haggai. They had also now got 'back to basics', and were positioned to hear Zechariah's further messages, enabling them to see God's bigger picture.

Discussion Starters

1. What was significant in the message "'Return to me,"
    declares the LORD Almighty' (v3) in terms of what it
    revealed about God and the response that He required?

    _____
    _____
    _____
    _____

2. What was important about the reminder that God had
    been 'very angry' (v2) with their ancestors?

    _____
    _____
    _____
    _____

3. God's declaration ended with 'and I will return to you' (v3),
    what did He mean by that (v16; also 2 Chron. 7:12–14)?

    _____
    _____
    _____
    _____

4. The message, 'Turn from your evil ways and... practices'
    (v4), had been previously brought to the ancestors of
    God's people. What was important about this message
    and still applicable for those hearing via Zechariah?

    _____
    _____
    _____
    _____

5. What was significant about the Jewish people's response: 'The LORD Almighty has done to us what our ways and practices deserve' (v6)?

_____

_____

_____

_____

6. How did John the Baptist sum up his message of repentance, and what action did he prescribe (Luke 3:7–14)?

_____

_____

_____

_____

7. The Laodiceans also needed to repent (Rev. 3:14–22). What similar response was required by the Laodiceans (v22) and the Jewish people (Zech. 1:4b)? Why was this integral to repentance?

_____

_____

_____

_____

8. From what did those Laodicean Christians need to repent? How can that apply to us?

_____

_____

_____

_____

Personal Application

Whatever various skills and abilities we possess – and in whatever sphere they may operate – there is always the requirement to have the basic competencies in place. The same goes for our spiritual being. Until we fully repent, receive forgiveness and aim to change, we cannot be in a place of close relationship with God and experience His purposes in our lives. The apostle John wrote of the need to acknowledge and confess sin (1 John 1:1–10). Getting the basics in place by addressing sin and forgiveness at the start of his first letter was clearly a prerequisite to opening up the truth about Jesus and God's love.

Seeing Jesus in the Scriptures

Jesus' ministry had benefitted from the preparatory work of John the Baptist, who had been forthright in underlining the need for his hearers to turn to God in repentance before they could experience a right relationship with Him: 'Produce fruit in keeping with repentance... I baptise you with water for repentance. But after me comes one who is more powerful than I... He will baptise you with the Holy Spirit and fire' (Matt. 3:8,11). Jesus' first message linked with that of John's: 'Repent, for the kingdom of heaven has come near' (Matt. 4:17). This 'back to basics' message was clearly grasped by Simon Peter who could only contemplate being a disciple of Jesus after he had acknowledged that he was a 'sinful man' (Luke 5:8).

WEEK TWO

Broadening our perspective

Opening Icebreaker

Search and print out from the internet (or use a hardcopy of the *The Highway Code*) a selection of different traffic signs found on roads in the UK. Discuss elements of the signs that make them understandable. Why is it important that they are distinguishable?

Bible Readings

- Zechariah 1:7–6:8 (if limited by time, 4:1–14)
- Psalm 138
- Ephesians 1:17–18
- Philippians 1:1–6
- Colossians 1:9–12

Opening Our Eyes

It was an unusual setting for familiar words found inscribed on a memorial stone of a restored railway station. Marking Ralph Povey's presidency of the Keighley & Worth Valley Railway Preservation Society, the inscription included the words: 'all things are possible for those who believe'. The inscription also explained that this man's 'quiet genius inspired the saving of this railway for future generations'. The Gospel writer Mark would not have envisaged those words of Jesus adapted to describe the efforts of this dedicated gentleman. But the general idea was valid. Mr Povey believed what others failed to envisage: steam trains running again in rural Yorkshire.

Envisioned

How this railway preservation enthusiast was able to foresee the restored line is not disclosed. But the memorial plaque shows that, even in a non-spiritual environment, people are able to visualise beyond their physical setting. The prophet Zechariah experienced this 'seeing' in a vivid way. The opening six chapters of his prophecy recount eight consecutive visions, initially during the night-time but subsequently when 'awakened from sleep' (Zech. 4:1). Many of his visions are prefaced, 'Then I looked up', followed by, 'and there before me' (1:18; 2:1; 5:1; 6:1). Each vision involved an explanation of what Zechariah was seeing, mainly given by the 'angel of the LORD' (1:11) (possibly indicating Jesus prior to His incarnation).

Understanding

Four aspects of what Zechariah was experiencing are important to note. Firstly, it was God's prerogative to communicate to the prophet by means of these visions. It was not something that Zechariah initiated or demanded. He made clear that God gave him these revelations: 'The

word of the LORD came to the prophet... During the night I
had a vision' (1:7,8). Secondly, these visions included familiar
and recognisable imagery. It would not have been out of
the ordinary for him to have seen horses (1:8), horns (1:18),
a measuring line (2:1), a turban (3:5), a lampstand (4:2), a
scroll (5:1), a basket (5:6) and chariots (6:1). Admittedly the
attendant features involving these articles were highly
unusual; for example, a flying scroll (5:1)!

But the unexpected circumstances surrounding those normal
items pointed to a third aspect. Zechariah needed God's help
to understand what he was being shown. He didn't pretend
to be able to interpret, nor was he prepared to gloss over the
images presented to him. Lastly, they indicated God clearly
intervening in the affairs of this world, most pointedly with
regard to His people, the Jews. Together, these four aspects
made a huge impact on Zechariah.

Intervention
The fifth vision (Zech. 4:1–14) underlined what God wanted
Zechariah to grasp. The Jews had returned from exile but
failed to rebuild the Temple. Haggai was instrumental in
bringing God's word to motivate His people to re-engage in
this work but obstacles, obstinacy and weariness weighed
heavily against completion. So Zechariah's initial striking
image involving a lampstand (symbolising the nation of
Israel) was designed to bring specific envisioning. The
governor, Zerubbabel, was seen holding a 'capstone' (v7) to
put into place as the last stage of the building process. God's
word accompanying this powerful image clearly pointed to
divine intervention: '"Not by might nor by power, but by my
Spirit," says the LORD Almighty' (4:6). God wanted Zechariah
to see more than a construction site. His perspective needed
to be broadened to see the completed Temple – the bigger
picture of God's purposes being fulfilled.

Discussion Starters

1. In what ways are we absorbed in situations immediately confronting us, rather than broadening our focus to see and grasp God's bigger perspective for us?

2. How do Zechariah's visions help to widen our focus on what God wants for us?

3. What was important about the vision of Joshua being accused by Satan and then given new clothes (Zech. 3:1–5)? How does it relate to us?

4. Why was Zechariah challenged about daring to 'despise the day of small things' (Zech. 4:10)? What refocusing did the rest of that verse bring? How can that apply to us?

5. What qualities of God are described in Zechariah 1:13,16,17? Why was it important to have these described?

6. Why is God named as 'LORD Almighty' (Zech. 1:12,14,16)?

7. What was Paul specifically praying for, regarding the Ephesian Christians (Eph. 1:17–18)? Why is this prayer relevant to us?

8. What assurances does the psalmist bring concerning God working in our lives (Psa. 138:8)? How does this compare with Paul's statement (Phil. 1:6)?

Personal Application

These visions describing God's interaction in the affairs of His people were aimed at broadening Zechariah's understanding. They brought God's perspective upon the current dejected state of the Jewish people and their future. The Israelites were not in a good frame of mind so the fifth vision (4:1–14) involved bringing encouragement – something we all need at times. The Jews saw an impossible task ahead of them in terms of rebuilding the Temple. But God was opening their eyes, through the prophet, to show them that the intervention of His Spirit would enable the work to be completed (vv6–10). Paul's prayer for the Christians in Colossae, that God would enlarge their spiritual perspective and fill them 'with the knowledge of his will through all the wisdom and understanding that the Spirit gives' (Col. 1:9), also applies to us.

Seeing Jesus in the Scriptures

The fourth vision (Zech. 3:1–10) was symbolic of the work of Jesus. It depicted 'Joshua the high priest standing before the angel of the LORD, and Satan standing at his right side to accuse him' (v1). The angel commands that Joshua's filthy clothes be replaced by 'fine garments' and 'clean turban' (vv4–5). Those new clothes point to the robe of righteousness that Christ's death has enabled us to wear (Isa. 61:10; 2 Cor. 5:21). The vision concludes with Joshua being 'symbolic of things to come', and 'the Branch' (Zech. 3:8) pointing to Jesus the Messiah (Isa. 11:1–5; Jer. 23:5–6). The 'stone' (Zech. 3:9) set before Joshua also depicted Jesus, the 'cornerstone' (Psa. 118:22; Acts 4:11).

WEEK THREE

Bringing focus

Opening Icebreaker

Discuss jobs or roles that require wearing a uniform or special clothing. To what extent is the clothing integral to the actual tasks that have to be performed? If not integral, what purpose do the items worn actually serve?

Bible Readings

- Zechariah 6:9–15
- Acts 13:1–3
- Romans 6:1–10
- 1 Corinthians 11:17–34

Opening Our Eyes

The option for viewers or listeners to be interactive is a key component of today's media scene. As well as phone-in radio programmes, you can voice your opinion via text, email or be part of a live audience for TV shows and debates. Then, of course, there is social media, which is generated and perpetuated by contributions by anyone and everyone in the form of comments, videos and photos.

Precise instructions
Twenty-first century communication is easy, fast and two-way. The prophet Zechariah, back in 519 BC, was given a particular message from God that required a response and action. Following the phrase, 'The word of the LORD came to me' (Zech. 6:9) was a set of precise instructions. He was told to craft a crown, place it on the head of Joshua the high priest and tell him: 'Here is the man whose name is the Branch, and he will branch out from his place and build the temple of the LORD' (v12).

This action would have particularly stood out because priests and kings were appointed from within two different Jewish tribes. No priest was ever recorded in the Old Testament as being king. The one king who took upon himself the role of priest (Uzziah) was severely judged by God (see 2 Chron. 26:26–21).

Powerful communication
The significance of God's message and instructions to Zechariah hinted at the work of the coming Lord Jesus who was to be revealed as both high priest and Lord of all. Jesus would be the one who would 'build the temple of the LORD' (v12), meaning the worldwide Church. Some commentators consider that this also points to a yet further reconstruction of the Temple – the previous one having been destroyed by

the Romans – that will then be in place immediately prior to Christ's second coming. Both Jews and Gentiles ('Those who are far away') would come to 'help to build the temple of the LORD' (v15) and the high priest (Jesus) would be 'clothed in majesty and will sit and rule on his throne' (v13).

Carrying out God's instruction was a powerful means of communication both for Zechariah and for the Jews. They needed to have a visual aid to help them understand God's future plans. This was not the first time God spoke by means of dramatic action. Jeremiah was directed to buy a field that was in enemy hands to confirm God's promise that His people would have their land restored (Jer. 32). Hosea was told to marry a woman who would be unfaithful to him, showing God's love to His wayward people (Hosea 1). Ezekiel was instructed to pack his bags to go on a journey, revealing God's intention that He would allow His people to be taken into exile (Ezek. 12).

Prophetic action
Does God still speak by means of prophetic action? A local church with which I was involved sensed that God was telling the members to form a human chain between the church and a separate hall. This was seen as a prophetic act, bringing into focus a possible plan to construct an atrium connecting the two buildings – something that was eventually accomplished in a subsequent redevelopment.

Discussion Starters

1. What extra impact does a message have when it is communicated by actions? What familiar stories from Genesis and Exodus illustrate this impact?

_____

_____

_____

_____

2. What was the importance of involving others in this visual message (Zech. 6:10,14)?

_____

_____

_____

_____

3. What was the purpose of that crown being a 'memorial' (v14)?

_____

_____

_____

_____

4. What was the reason for the action (the crown put on the head of Joshua) being accompanied by a verbal explanation (vv12–13)?

_____

_____

_____

_____

5. Why was the phrase 'build the temple of the LORD' repeated (vv12,13,15)? What is the significance of God saying something that He had previously spoken about?

_____

_____

_____

_____

6. What was the significance of a priest being on his throne (v13) in terms of it being a portrayal of Jesus?

_____

_____

_____

_____

7. What examples are there of Jesus using actions as well as words when He was teaching?

_____

_____

_____

_____

8. How can we be more sensitive and aware of God speaking to us through actions, sights and other non-verbal means?

_____

_____

_____

_____

Personal Application

Celebrating and remembering God's work in our lives through visible actions are particularly evident in respect of Holy Communion (1 Cor. 11:17–34) and baptism (Rom. 6:1–10). These are not simply symbolic acts and a testimony to onlookers of our relationship with Jesus. They also involve a powerful spiritual dynamic concerning Christ's atoning death and our new life in Him. Other New Testament church practices can also apply. These include the laying on of hands (with prayer) for a particular calling or gifting from God (Acts 13:3; 2 Tim. 1:6), and anointing the sick with oil for healing (James 5:14). These involve bringing a focus on God's bigger picture for our lives, communicated in a clear, outward form.

Seeing Jesus in the Scriptures

This entire passage is aimed at bringing a focus on Jesus the Messiah. God's clear instruction to Zechariah was designed to make the prophet's contemporaries take notice and consider what was taking place in front of their eyes, symbolic of a coronation. Those Jews' attention had been centred on their environment, having had to rebuild their lives after returning from exile. The initial prophetic message from Haggai had been geared to their physical surroundings of rebuilding the Temple. But with this extraordinary act of setting a crown on the priest's head, together with those Messianic terms of being named 'the Branch' and 'clothed with majesty', their attention was dramatically shifted. There was no mistaking God's plans confirming the coming Messiah, uniting kingship with priesthood – 'harmony between the two' (v13).

WEEK FOUR
Blessings and encouragement

Opening Icebreaker

Examine the adverts in a selection of magazines, and list the features that are designed to entice people to buy a particular product or service.

Bible Readings

- Zechariah 8:1–23
- Mark 4:35–5:43
- 1 Thessalonians 5:12–18
- 2 Thessalonians 2:16–17

Opening Our Eyes

An experienced church pastor wrote: 'I have a theory that most Christians face discouragement so often that when encouragement comes along we are not sure how to handle it. We look at our feet and think: "Are they talking to me?"'* The causes of discouragement are numerous and ongoing. Advertisements bombard us with messages about our defective and inadequate state, remedied by the products they promote.

The Jewish people at the time of Zechariah had reasons for feeling discouraged. They were now a small and powerless group, and the homeland to which they had returned was devastated and surrounded by enemies. They had struggled to obey God's instructions to reconstruct the Temple and institute worship. Their history showed persistent waywardness from God – would they ever get back on track?

Indicative of their current poor spiritual outlook was their question: Do we still need to fast now that we are no longer in exile (Zech. 7:1–3)? God's response through Zechariah was to reveal their self-centred motives and mistaken equating of spirituality with outward performance only (vv4–7). A change of heart to love others was needed (vv8–10).

'Full-on' blessings

This lack of love and hardness of heart towards God made Him 'very angry' (v12) and the Israelites were 'scattered… among all the nations' (v14). God was pointing to His earlier dismembering of the northern kingdom, a salutary reminder of His anger. But then, after almost two years of God being silent (Zech. 1:7; 7:1), there is an amazing outburst of affection and blessing from God for His downtrodden and discouraged people. Ten messages of 'full-on' blessings are given, each prefaced with: 'This is what the LORD Almighty says'

(Zech. 8:2,3,4,6,7,9,14,19,20,23). The first is an unequivocal declaration of His intense and consuming love for His people: 'I am burning with jealousy for her' (v2), seen alongside God's earlier statement that they are 'the apple of his eye' (Zech. 2:8).

Moving up the gears

God then declares ways in which His love is evidenced. It's as though He is 'moving up the gears' as He proclaims He 'will return to Zion and dwell in Jerusalem' (Zech. 8:3), giving a sense of safety to the vulnerable and protection for His returning people. He then reassures them that He is no longer angry and He 'will not deal with the remnant of this people as I did in the past' (v11). Instead there would be an abundance of agricultural produce and His people would be a blessing to others (vv9–13).

Broken boundaries

These successive blessings then take on a distinct spiritual dimension. Since God has now 'determined to do good' (v15), His people need not be afraid and should treat one another in a godly way. The evidence of God's blessing and presence would draw outsiders to seek Him through the witness and testimony of His people (vv20–22). Boundaries would be broken; non-Jews would be drawn to God: 'Let us go with you, because we have heard that God is with you' (v23).

The start of Zechariah's prophecy included him hearing 'kind and comforting words' (Zech. 1:13). Now God had brought 'marvellous' encouragement (Zech. 8:6) to all His people and also promises concerning 'many peoples… all languages and nations' (vv22,23). 'In those days' (v23) points to a marvellously transformed spiritual environment that will be orchestrated by God when He brings His people back to Jerusalem.

*John Benton, 'The Ten Encouragements', posted May 2003, taken from evangelical-times.org [Accessed December 2019]

Discussion Starters

1. Why was it important that God's blessings to His people start with affirming words (Zech. 8:1–3,8)?

2. Why was it also important that God promised to bless His people in a practical way (v12)?

3. What was the purpose of God specifically instructing His people to let their hands 'be strong' (v13)?

4. How can the blessings concerning peoples and nations coming to Jerusalem 'to seek the LORD Almighty' be applicable to us (vv20–23)?

5. Looking at the reading from Mark 4:35–5:43, what were some of the pressing situations that caused Jesus to reach out and bring encouragement? What does that tell us about our relationship with Jesus?

_____

_____

_____

_____

6. Discuss the different forms of encouragement that Jesus used in Mark 4:35–5:43.

_____

_____

_____

_____

7. What did the apostle Paul say about the blessing of God's encouragement (2 Thess. 2:16–17)?

_____

_____

_____

_____

8. What blessing does the act of encouragement bring in our lives as Christians (1 Thess. 5:12–18)?

_____

_____

_____

_____

Personal Application

The blessings and encouragement described by Zechariah
in respect of God's intervention in the lives of His people
are a wonderful reminder to ourselves of His character.
God's purposes and personhood do not change; His attitude
towards His people at that time is still true for us today. God
has promised to never leave us, to bring restoration, to be
our heavenly Father, to provide our needs and many other
unmerited blessings. Just like the Jews of old, we consistently
fall short of all that God desires us to be but He doesn't give up
on us. His determination 'to do good again to Jerusalem and
Judah' (Zech. 8:15) also extends to us (v22).

Seeing Jesus in the Scriptures

God's blessings, described by Zechariah, included Him twice
telling His people: 'Do not be afraid' (Zech. 8:13,15). Jesus
also encouraged His followers with similar words during His
ministry; for instance, when He came to them in their boat,
walking on the water: 'Take courage! It is I. Don't be afraid'
(Matt. 14:27). Another time, when He was transfigured, He
spoke these words to Peter, James and John: '"Get up," he
said. "Don't be afraid"' (Matt. 17:7). Encouragement featured
in the words to Peter at his commissioning: 'Don't be afraid;
from now on you will fish for people' (Luke 5:10). And when
sending out His disciples, there was a similar encouragement:
'So don't be afraid; you are worth more than many sparrows'
(Matt. 10:31).

WEEK FIVE

Brought back

Opening Icebreaker

List the possible steps that are needed in order to find
something that has been lost or misplaced at home.

Bible Readings

- Zechariah 9:1–10:12
- Psalm 2
- Psalm 118:22–23
- Ephesians 1
- 1 Peter 1

Opening Our Eyes

A significant event took place in December 1917 when General Allenby, commanding the allied forces in the Middle East, walked into Jerusalem through the Jaffa Gate, marking the end of many centuries of Ottoman-Turkish rule over Palestine. It presaged the return of Jews to their homeland in unprecedented numbers. Having a population of around 50,000 in 1900, by 1948 when the State of Israel was declared it was 650,000 – it is now over 9 million.*

The survival of the Jews and returning to their homeland were consistent features of biblical prophecy. (Persecution by the Russians, Poles and Nazis in recent history highlights their continuing perilous situation.) However, God's overruling action in these events was the dominant factor.

God's future plans

Against the backdrop of God's people's recent experiences in Babylonian exile and being brought back home, Zechariah now receives a 'burden' (the Hebrew meaning of 'prophecy'; 9:1, KJV) concerning God's bigger picture: His future plans both relatively soon and far ahead.

It is generally agreed that Zechariah's opening section (9:1–8) describes the future conquests of Alexander the Great in that part of the Middle East, following his victory over the Persian Empire (the superpower at the time of Zechariah) in 333 BC. In particular, there is a clear prophecy regarding God's protection of His people in respect of this invasion (9:8). This was confirmed by the historian Flavius Josephus (*The Antiquities of the Jews*, xi.8.3).

Christ's coming

Zechariah then shifts his perspective and the well-known verse appears: 'See, your king comes to you... riding on a

donkey' (Zech. 9:9), relating to the event of Palm Sunday
(around AD 30). The Gospel writers clearly link their
description of Christ's entry into Jerusalem to this prophecy
(Matt. 21:4–5; John 12:14–15). However, the next verse
(Zech. 9:10) takes a massive step further into the future in
describing His second coming in power: 'He will proclaim
peace to the nations. His rule will extend from sea to sea.'

The following section (vv11–13) is unclear to commentators.
Some consider it as referring to the Jewish (Maccabean)
rebellion against the Greeks. Others indicate that these verses,
and chapter 10, are entirely symbolic, describing a wholly
spiritual scenario. However, there are those who regard these
verses as describing actual events that are yet to take place.
These events involve God's people returning from yet another
exile ('prisoners' 9:11,12). God's powerful protection of His
people (9:14–17) is shown through the coming of the Messiah
to 'save his people on that day' (9:16).

Further exile
Chapter 10 further describes how God will intervene, look
after His people and be like a shepherd caring 'for his flock,
the people of Judah' (v3; see also 9:16). God promises to bring
them back from 'Egypt' and 'Assyria' and, as a consequence,
there will 'not be room enough for them' in the land (v10).
This is an important feature to consider. Having already been
in captivity, specifically in Babylon, can this further exile
(in Egypt and Assyria) be Zechariah's description of events
following the Roman's destruction of Jerusalem in AD 70 and
the Jews being forced away from their homeland? Almost
two millennia later, General Allenby's entry into Jerusalem,
and the provision it made for the Jews to return home and
subsequently become an independent nation state, may
contribute towards the fulfilment of this prophetic passage.

*jewishvirtuallibrary.org

Discussion Starters

1. What general difficulties are we likely to have when reading biblical prophecy?

_____

_____

_____

_____

2. The reference to the emergence of the Greek Empire (and the looming Roman Empire of the New Testament) points to secular history merging with God's plans and purposes. How did the existence of these empires contribute to the eventual spread of the gospel?

_____

_____

_____

_____

3. What words and phrases are used in Zechariah 9 and 10 to describe God's character regarding His specific care of His people?

_____

_____

_____

_____

4. What further words and phrases in these chapters describe His power?

_____

_____

_____

_____

5. What relevance do these descriptions of God's care and
    power have on us as Christians (see 1 Pet. 1:1–9)?

    _____

    _____

    _____

    _____

6. Why did God instruct His people to 'Ask the LORD for
    rain in the springtime' (Zech. 10:1), and how does that
    apply to us?

    _____

    _____

    _____

    _____

7. What phrases in Zechariah chapters 9 and 10 describe
    God's intervention in bringing His people back to
    their homeland again? What was the purpose of such
    specific prophecy?

    _____

    _____

    _____

    _____

8. Despite the challenging content, why is it important
    for these chapters (and those that follow) to be read
    and studied?

    _____

    _____

    _____

    _____

Personal Application

Although these two chapters of Zechariah are difficult to grasp and will generate differing viewpoints, there are aspects that are applicable today. They show that God is active in this world now, in the past and the future. Despite political and societal changes we witness around us, it is reassuring to know that He is powerfully at work: 'His rule will extend from sea to sea' (Zech. 9:10). God wants us to be aware and focused on what He is doing. He had previously spoken of revealing His plans (Amos 3:7) and these verses describe Him talking about His people seeing His work (9:9; 10:7). This was also Paul's prayer (Eph. 1:15–23). Lastly, seeing God's bigger picture encourages our praise: 'their hearts will be glad as with wine… joyful… rejoice' (10:7).

Seeing Jesus in the Scriptures

Several portrayals of Jesus arise in Zechariah 9 and 10. Having previously alluded to God being the shepherd of His people (cf Jesus spoke of Himself being the good shepherd, John 10:14), it is then stated: 'From Judah will come the cornerstone, from him the tent peg, from him the battle-bow, from him every ruler' (Zech. 10:4). The cornerstone speaks of Christ as the foundation for His people, the keystone that joins the walls (Psa. 118:22; 1 Pet. 2:7). The tent peg refers to Him as one on whom burdens may be confidently placed (Isa. 22:20–24), and 'battle-bow' as Him being all-powerful. Lastly, He is the absolute ruler (Psa. 2).

WEEK SIX

Broken staffs

Opening Icebreaker

Discuss what is meant by the term 'shepherding' when used in a general sense, not just in the context of sheep. How might this approach differ from that of a politician or the police?

Bible Readings

- Zechariah 11
- Psalm 23
- John 10:1–18

Opening Our Eyes

The news channels provide daily proof that we live in a harsh, confusing and sometimes frightening world where good leadership is often absent. Zechariah's times were no different. He did not hold back in bringing God's prophetic word to His people, especially in the crucial area of leadership.

Shepherding

Zechariah was instructed by God to speak about the role of a shepherd. (He may even have acted it out.) The implications of this would have been understood by his immediate audience. God's people were the 'flock' being led by 'shepherds'. However, the scenario being presented was not restricted to that particular point in time. This is one of many occasions in the Old Testament where the timing of events being described can shift quite dramatically. In this case, the initial context was of the shepherds, or leaders of God's people, wailing on account of the devastating invasion of their land (Zech. 11:1–3). This is generally accepted as referring to the future Roman occupation of Israel.

Staffs

Zechariah, referring to the role of a shepherd, then specifically describes the use and subsequent breaking of shepherd staffs. A shepherd would usually have two staffs: one was short and thick, used to beat off attacking animals, and the other was long and thin with a curve at one end designed to reach and retrieve errant sheep. In Zechariah's case, one staff was called 'Favour' and the other 'Union' (v7). They both ended up being dramatically broken, giving a clear warning since these staffs were essential to the protection of the flock.

The breaking of the first staff is considered to relate to God withdrawing His favour from the Jews following their rejection (and crucifixion) of Jesus as indicated by those words of Zechariah, 'The flock detested me' (v8). Then followed the totally destructive invasion by the Romans under Vespasian and Titus in AD 70. The 'thirty pieces of silver' thrown to 'the potter' (v13) was referenced by Matthew in his account of Jesus' betrayal by Judas (Matt. 26:14–15; 27:9), though he quoted it as being from Jeremiah. The breaking of the second staff, 'Union', (Zech. 11:14) portrayed the nation, divided many years previously, now fragmenting even further on account of this lack of protective leadership.

Foolish

Finally, Zechariah was told to 'Take again the equipment of a foolish shepherd' (v15). 'Foolish' in this context meant a morally deficient and corrupt shepherd who would show total disdain towards the 'sheep' under their care. This prophecy signified that God's people would experience extreme adversity under such leadership, resulting in some commentators concluding that this is an oblique reference to the antichrist, becoming prominent many years ahead.

As with other prophetic sections of the Bible, these words and enactments (breaking of the staffs) of Zechariah raise questions and differing viewpoints. But there is no doubt as to the effect of the vivid representation of this message on God's people at that time. Their history presented clear evidence of their tendency to act like sheep. They persisted in wandering away from God and His purposes for them. Their failure to fully follow God warranted His severe discipline as indicated by the breaking of those staffs by Zechariah, with future leadership being abusive and destructive.

Discussion Starters

1. What does the repeated wailing, as described in verses 2–3, indicate?

_____

_____

_____

_____

2. Why is the term 'flock' used to describe God's people (vv4,7,8,11,17)?

_____

_____

_____

_____

3. What is notable about Moses, David and Amos, prior to them being appointed as leaders/prophets (Exod. 3:1; 1 Sam. 16:11–13; Amos 7:14)?

_____

_____

_____

_____

4. Although there are negative terms in chapter 11, what do the phrases 'the LORD my God says... declares the LORD... the LORD said' (vv4,6,13,15) all indicate?

_____

_____

_____

_____

5. What do the actions of that 'foolish shepherd' particularly show regarding his attitude towards God's people (vv15–16)?

_____

_____

_____

_____

6. What is striking about the words of the Jewish religious leaders in rejecting Jesus (as prophesied by Zechariah) when presenting their case to Pilate, and putting another in His place (John 19:12–15)?

_____

_____

_____

_____

7. What was the significance of the prophetic message regarding the value (30 pieces of silver) placed upon the 'shepherd' by God's people as relating to Jesus (Zech. 11:12–13; see also Exod. 21:32; Matt. 26:14–15)?

_____

_____

_____

_____

8. How did God want His people to view Him (Psa. 78:52–55; 80:1–2)?

_____

_____

_____

_____

Personal Application

Zechariah needed his audience to grasp the bigger picture of God's work and character. This involved seeing the stark contrast between good and 'foolish' shepherding, and how their own attitude towards the shepherd was important. The dramatic breaking of the two shepherd staffs showed the consequences of rejecting God's leadership. For our own benefit, we also need to fully submit to God's tender care and shepherding of us. The psalmist described the wonderful care that God provides (Psa. 23) and Isaiah described His tenderness: 'he gathers the lambs in his arms and carries them close to his heart' (Isa. 40:11). The words of the prophet Isaiah remind us of the need to closely follow God and of not going astray (Isa. 53:6).

Seeing Jesus in the Scriptures

God instructed Zechariah to enact the role of a shepherd (vv4,7), clearly representing Jesus' ministry when on earth. Jesus Himself was described as having compassion on people 'because they were harassed and helpless, like sheep without a shepherd' (Matt. 9:36). This extended to a Canaanite woman whose daughter was 'demon possessed and suffering terribly' (Matt. 15:22). When Jesus said to her that He was 'sent only to the lost sheep of Israel' (Matt. 15:24), her reply of faith, and Jesus' healing of her daughter, showed that His sheep included *all* those who believed.

Jesus clearly declared: 'I am the good shepherd' (John 10:14). The extent of His care was that He 'lay down [His] life for the sheep' (v15).

WEEK SEVEN

Beyond the horizon

Opening Icebreaker

Compile a list of technical devices that would not have been in use 60 years ago (eg smartphones, tablets, laptops). Discuss the extent to which science fiction has predicted the technologies we now utilise.

Bible Readings

- Zechariah 12–14
- Matthew 24:30–44
- 2 Peter 3:1–14

Opening Our Eyes

A little-known rail route across north London includes tracks running on viaducts constructed over roads and above the level of surrounding houses. This means that stretches of the line and one particular station are particularly exposed to weather conditions, as I discovered waiting for a train early one winter morning. The gloom and mist meant that nothing was seen of the approaching train until it suddenly emerged at the end of the platform – to my relief and that of other expectant passengers.

The closing chapters of Zechariah bring images relating to the future. Not only were they beyond the horizon of the prophet's audience, but even for ourselves the prophecies have yet to be fulfilled.

However, a phrase used 15 times in this section points to significant situations: 'On that day' (eg Zech. 12:3,4,6). The events surrounding that 'day' may not be easy to understand but, like my train, clarity will eventually emerge.

Jesus' return...

Some details, however, are discernible. Firstly, and most importantly, is that they relate to the return of the Lord Jesus to this world. 'On that day his feet will stand on the Mount of Olives, east of Jerusalem' (Zech. 14:4). These words have a link with the words of the angels to the watching disciples at Jesus' ascension from Bethany (on the Mount of Olives): 'why do you stand here looking into the sky? This same Jesus, who has been taken from you into heaven, will come back in the same way you have seen him go into heaven' (Acts 1:11).

... as King...

Secondly, Jesus will return in power and glory in contrast to His incarnation as a helpless baby. 'The LORD will be king over the whole earth. On that day there will be one LORD, and his name the only name' (Zech. 14:9). He will have the pre-eminence in everything: 'On that day HOLY TO THE LORD will be inscribed on the bells of the horses, and the cooking pots in the LORD's house will be like the sacred bowls in front of the altar' (v20).

Thirdly, there will be cataclysmic events surrounding His return. The images presented by Zechariah are not clear but do convey the sense of unmistakable and extraordinary circumstances: 'On that day there will be neither sunlight nor cold, frosty darkness. It will be a unique day – a day known only to the LORD – with no distinction between day and night. When evening comes, there will be light. On that day living water will flow out from Jerusalem, half of it east to the Dead Sea and half of it west to the Mediterranean Sea, in summer and in winter' (vv6–8).

... to intervene

These events will be interwoven with God's people experiencing divine intervention, which has been a particular focus for debate with some people thinking that these chapters specifically refer to the Jews and a literal Jerusalem. Israel's re-emergence as a nation state is a considerable factor in taking these verses as they stand. Jesus' return marks His intervention in what would otherwise be a totally disastrous invasion by Israel's enemies.

Finally, these chapters point to God bringing tremendous spiritual revival. 'On that day a fountain will be opened to the house of David and the inhabitants of Jerusalem, to cleanse them from sin and impurity' (Zech. 13:1; also see 13:2,4; 14:16). However imperfect our present understanding, these images point us to God's bigger picture for this world and ourselves as we await their fulfilment.

Discussion Starters

1. What do the verses containing the phrase 'On that day...' point to regarding God's power?

2. Why did Zechariah begin this final section with those words 'The LORD, who stretches out the heavens' (Zech. 12:1)?

3. In what way do the details contained in Zechariah chapters 12–14 reflect God's control over the situations leading up to Jesus' return?

4. What verses particularly show the degree of protection that God exercises over His people in the face of great trouble?

5. The words 'known only to the LORD' (Zech. 14:7) link with the words of Jesus, regarding the fact that no one knows the date of His return (Matt. 24:36). Why is it important to note that both Old and New Testament prophecies speak about His return but that no date is specified?

_____

_____

_____

_____

6. What particular warning is given in the reading from Matthew 24? How should we respond?

_____

_____

_____

_____

7. Why should we note the further details given in these two prophecies regarding the manner in which Jesus will return (see Matt. 24:30–31; Zech. 14:3–4,9)?

_____

_____

_____

_____

8. What description does Peter bring that is also brought by Zechariah (2 Pet. 3:10–13)?

_____

_____

_____

_____

Personal Application

The closing words of this prophecy point to a time when the holiness of God is emphasised as not only being a factor in Temple worship but integral to ordinary life: 'Every pot in Jerusalem and Judah will be holy to the LORD Almighty' (Zech. 14:21). Peter, writing to New Testament Christians, instructs his readers that holiness needs to be our response to this entire scenario regarding Christ's return. 'You ought to live holy and godly lives as you look forward to the day of God and speed its coming... make every effort to be found spotless, blameless and at peace with him' (2 Pet. 3:11–12,14). Seeing God's bigger picture challenges us to live in a way that is distinctive. Are you and I focusing beyond the horizon?

Seeing Jesus in the Scriptures

The last two chapters of Zechariah centre on Jesus Himself and His return in glory to this earth. One of the verses, 'I will strike the shepherd, and the sheep of the flock will be scattered' (Zech. 13:7), is subsequently quoted by Jesus in two of the Gospels (Matt. 26:31; Mark 14:27). Jesus took these words as applying to Himself, His arrest and crucifixion with the consequent abandonment by His disciples; 'This very night you will all fall away on account of me' (Matt. 26:31). Whereas those disciples were subsequently restored after the resurrection, the scattering of the Jews as a whole (following the Roman invasion of AD 70) meant that it was almost 2,000 years before the Jewish people were regathered in Israel.

Leader's Notes

Opening Icebreaker

Most self-assembly items come with a printed instruction sheet to be read through first, especially if any safety precautions need to be taken. Then you need to check that all the components are provided and that you have the necessary tools or equipment required for assembly. These are the basic initial steps to enable construction of the item.

Aim of the Session

To understand that true repentance and receiving forgiveness from God is the basis for seeing and experiencing the bigger picture of His work and plans for the future.

Discussion Starters

1. God's message showed that He really wanted His people to repent and return to Him. Not only did He take specific action to bring those words through Zechariah but He added 'and I will return to you' (Zech. 1:3). This pointed to the closer relationship He wanted arising from the people's clear and unequivocal change.

2. The fact that God had been 'very angry' (v2) was a reminder that He was not a dispassionate, impartial or passive observer to what He had seen taking place regarding His people. He was very aware of both outward actions and inner attitudes. Holy anger had been evident in God's action regarding the Jews being taken into exile (2 Chron. 7:19–21).

3. Essentially God promised to bless His people and bring 'mercy' (Zech. 1:16). God's response to Solomon's prayer at

the dedication of the Temple many centuries previously included a promise to 'heal their land' (2 Chron. 7:14). Repeated use of His name 'LORD Almighty' (Zech. 1:3) underlined His authority and power to bring that blessing, mercy and healing about which He had spoken.

4. Specific action of turning (the original Hebrew word meant 'turning back') was being required by God in terms of His people clearly putting away their evil mindsets and actions.

5. The Jews honestly acknowledged their evil deeds, admitting that they had done wrong in God's sight and deserved His punishment. This is the essence of true confession (1 John 1:9).

6. John the Baptist summed up his message by saying 'Produce fruit in keeping with repentance' (Luke 3:8) and gave examples of specific actions to difference groups of people (vv11–14).

7. Both the Laodiceans and the Jewish people had been warned about the need to listen carefully to God's message (Zech. 1:4; Rev. 3:22). God was not only drawing attention to sin but describing the consequences of failing to respond. Listening carefully was necessary in order to fully acknowledge that what God was saying was true; He was the 'Amen' (Rev. 3:14).

8. The Laodiceans held a sense of self-sufficiency and complacency in their lives, being influenced by their affluent society. In materially prosperous areas and countries, there might be the same tendency for Christians to have an ambivalent attitude towards God and their relationship with Him. This had been the basic problem that Haggai had identified with regard to

the Jews at the time when both he and Zechariah were bringing God's word to the people (Hag. 1:4).

Week Two: Broadening our perspective

Opening Icebreaker

Road signs are understandable as they are in simple and clear pictorial form – images without writing – indicating something more substantial.

They need to be immediately understandable because motorists may only have a moment's notice to recognise and respond to a hazard about which the road sign is warning.

Aim of the Session

To be aware that God wants to broaden our understanding of His plans and purposes – His bigger picture – and He does this by speaking to us in different ways.

Discussion Starters

1. Living in an environment where our physical senses are continually assailed, it is hard to 'see' beyond what our minds are being 'fed' from around us. In addition, our spiritual senses are 'blinded' by the forces of darkness (2 Cor. 4:4). The psalmist and Paul remind us respectively of the need to 'be still' to enable us to focus on God (Psa. 46:10; 2 Cor. 4:6,18).

2. Zechariah's visions help us realise that much more is going on than what we see in a physical sense. God is working in ways far outside our comprehension and expectations. Zechariah's visions also remind us that God is not limited in His power or love. He desires the best for us as He brings His glorious purposes into being. We are also made aware that God wants to communicate

His broader perspective to us; we are not spectators with regard to God's plans (Jer. 29:11–14).

3. The Jews were made to be very aware of their sinfulness; their 70-year exile was evidence of God's righteous discipline in that respect. But they were also made to realise the spiritually bad influence of the Babylonians. The vision was a powerful statement of God dealing with sin and then imputing righteousness. We are in a similar position in terms of our wilful sinfulness being compounded by our spiritually darkened environment. The New Testament confirms what God has done for us through Christ (1 Cor. 1:30; 2 Cor. 5:21; Rom. 3:22).

4. Many Israelites, including Zechariah, may have thought that efforts to rebuild the Temple were futile. They needed reminding that God had amazingly intervened to safely bring the Jews out of exile and back to their homeland where He'd protected them. God was clearly at work, so the Jews were not to dismiss their initial efforts. Those 'eyes of the LORD' (Zech. 4:10) symbolised God's watchful preserving power. We need reminding of God's ongoing work in our lives, however unpromising things may appear (Phil. 2:13).

5. God's characteristics listed in these verses – speaking kind and comforting words, being merciful, present with His people, bringing comfort – were encouragements regarding His care, needed after years of negativity and oppression.

6. Being named as 'LORD Almighty' (NIV) or 'LORD of hosts' (KJV) underlined God's supreme power at a time when the Jews were especially vulnerable and helpless.

7. Paul's prayer was about revelation, hope and perspective being broadened. Like the Ephesian Christians, and Jews at the time of Zechariah, we are living in spiritually dark days and need to be aware of God's work in and through us.

8. The psalmist is convinced that God will not abandon the work He has begun in his life. This is consistent with Paul's statement of God's intention to complete what He's begun in each of us.

Week Three: Bringing focus

Opening Icebreaker
People who wear uniforms include the police, paramedics, fire fighters, postal workers, courier employees, clergy and traffic enforcement personnel. Some elements of clothing are clearly necessary for the tasks being undertaken, such as hard hats worn by building site workers. Many elements of uniforms are designed to symbolise authority and qualifications.

Aim of the Session
To recognise that sometimes God works through symbolic outward actions to enable us to focus on His bigger picture.

Discussion Starters
1. Actions impact our visual senses (sometimes also our sense of touch), which help retain and recall what has been witnessed, making a greater impact than hearing alone. Examples of God communicating via actions are when He told Abraham to sacrifice Isaac (Gen 22:1–14) and when He instructed the Israelites to daub their doorposts with blood (Exod. 12:22–23).

2. The involvement of others would show that God was not restricting the means, or people, by which He wanted to convey His message. The Bible records many seemingly unlikely people (and a donkey!) who were instrumental in communicating a message from God.

3. The 'memorial' element of this action was for the crown to be retained and act as a tangible reminder of what God had said through Zechariah and this symbolic action. This was important for future generations to remember.

4. The verbal explanation of the crown being put on Joshua's head was to ensure that its significance was clearly and precisely understood. The action was God's way of underlining His plans for the future.

5. God's use of repetition is to put unmistakable emphasis on what He's said and to confirm His plans and purposes. The Temple would undoubtedly be built because God had said so more than once. (Pharaoh being given two similar dreams meant that the years of plenty and famine would definitely happen; see Gen. 41:32.) God's intention of the Temple being rebuilt points to His plans involving the return of Jesus Christ.

6. Jesus Christ is clearly described as being our high priest: the one who mediates on our behalf before the Father (Heb. 4:14; 5:5). His role in that respect was foreshadowed by Melchizedek (Gen. 14:18–20; Heb. 5:6; 7:1–3). Jesus is also clearly the one who is King of kings (Heb. 1:8–9). Zechariah prophesies of this combined role: 'And there will be harmony between the two' (Zech. 6:13).

7. Jesus' ministry involved several different ways of interaction in people's lives. He touched them (Mark 1:40–42), spat and then touched them

(Mark 7:33–35), brought them parables (Mark 4:1–8), pointed to what was around (Matt. 17:20), instructed His disciples to act in specific ways (Mark 6:7–13), and Himself acted out particular Old Testament prophecies (Matt. 21:1–5; relating to a prophecy in Zech. 9:9). All of these visual aids were aimed to help people understand and experience God's bigger picture.

8. God may choose to speak to us in a more demonstrative form, just as He did to Peter and Paul (Acts 10:9–20; 21:10–11). These two apostles needed to be focused on God's bigger picture, regarding what lay ahead. We also need to be careful not to dismiss these different means of God speaking to us (1 Thess. 5:19-22). Our own limitations in understanding God's ways need to be acknowledged and our dependence upon God deepened (Isa. 55:8–9; 1 Cor. 2:6–10).

Week Four: Blessings and encouragement

Opening Icebreaker
Most adverts project a dual message: pointing out the need that is met by their product or service and the deficiency or defectiveness that exists without it. The former is likely to involve highlighting superior or exciting aspects.

Aim of the Session
To show that God wants us to be aware of the bigger picture of His encouragement and blessings.

Discussion Starters
1. God needed to reassure His people that, although they were going through a time of spiritual and material challenges and uncertainty, He still loved them and had not given up

on them. He restated His commitment to be with them: 'I will return to Zion and dwell in Jerusalem' (Zech. 8:3).

2. The times leading up to Zechariah's prophecy had seen the homeland of God's people devastated by their enemies and subjected to drought, blight and infestation – means by which God had brought His discipline. The clear blessing of fruitfulness would show His specific and positive intervention: 'I will give all these things' (v12). It would also be a clear witness and even a blessing to outsiders (v13).

3. God knew that His people were particularly distracted and disheartened in terms of rebuilding the Temple due to difficulties they faced. They therefore needed encouragement (Hag. 2:2–5). Zechariah, having earlier brought encouragement to Zerubbabel the governor (Zech. 4:6-10), now encourages the Jews to rebuild the Temple and also to live godly lives (8:16–19).

4. These blessings from God relating to those who were not Jews confirm that anyone of any nationality, race or ethnicity can seek God, and that He desires that all peoples of this world come to know Him. Christ's commission reaffirmed our responsibility as Christians of making 'disciples of all nations' (Matt. 28:18–20). As part of this we need to remember that Paul explained that God's 'gifts and calls are irrevocable' (Rom. 11:29). This was in the context of the Jews still being integral to God's plans and a source of spiritual blessing to this world – a factor that some consider to point to end-time spiritual revival literally involving the Jews and Jerusalem as indicated in Zechariah 8.

5. The adverse conditions arising from the fierce storm, someone being demonically oppressed, a dead girl

and a chronic condition were all pressing situations that caused Jesus to intervene with words that brought encouragement and effected change. They illustrate that God can bring encouragement and blessing whatever our condition or situation

6. Jesus brought encouragement by showing compassion, power, insight and specific intervention.

7. Paul's words showed that God is aware of our need for encouragement and takes clear action to bring it. He sees encouragement as integral to us being able to do His will.

8. The act of encouragement, something that we can bring to one another as instructed by Paul, involves bringing warning, helping, being patient and striving to do good to one another.

Week Five: Brought back

Opening Icebreaker
A combination of steps might be necessary, such as trying to remember when the item was last seen or used, checking where it's normally kept, asking other members of the household about it, and searching in possible locations.

Aim of the Session
To understand that God's action in bringing His people back to their homeland is deliberate and an illustration of His intervention in our lives.

Discussion Starters
1. A lot of biblical prophecy is presented in pictorial form, which is not immediately relevant to our age and culture, describing actions, people groups and a geography with

which we are not familiar. Another factor is the shift in perspective, sometimes involving large periods of time, extending even beyond our current age.

2. The culture, language and power of the Greek Empire, and then the Roman Empire, acted as a massive unifying influence on vast areas and people groups of the then-known world. This resulted, for instance, in the New Testament epistles being written in the common Greek language of the first century and being widely readable. In addition, *Pax Romana* (a time of Roman peace) enabled Paul, amongst others, to travel widely in spreading the gospel.

3. Words and phrases include: 'encamp at my temple... guard it' (Zech. 9:8); 'free your prisoners' (v11); 'restore' (v12); 'shield' (v15); 'saves his flock' (v16); 'care for his flock' (10:3); and 'compassion' (v6).

4. Further words and phrases include: 'word... is against' (Zech. 9:1); 'take away' (v4); 'destroy' (v4) 'consumed' (v4); 'righteous and victorious' (v9); 'rule' (v10); 'arrow will flash like lightning' (v14); 'Sovereign LORD' (v14); and 'sends the thunderstorms... showers of rain' (10:1).

5. God's power and care are similarly directed towards those who are 'God's elect' and have 'new birth into a living hope' (1 Pet. 1:1,3). As a result of God's intervention we have an 'inheritance... kept in heaven' (v4); we are 'shielded by God's power' (v5); and we receive 'the end result of [our] faith, the salvation of [our] souls' (v9). This causes a response of 'joy' (1 Pet. 1:8; see Zech. 10:7).

6. Although God's plans and purposes were sometimes revealed through prophecies (including the blessings of good harvests as in Zech. 8:12), He instructed His people

to specifically pray to Him for these provisions in order that His people deepened their relationship with Him. God wants us to persevere in prayer so that we might know Him more intimately as our Father in heaven (Luke 11:5–13).

7. Phrases relating to God's plans to bring His people back to their homeland appear in Zechariah 9:11–12,16; 10:8–10. A period (consisting of centuries if viewing these words as describing the dispersion of the Jews following the Roman invasion of AD 70) of exile and oppression had seen God's people dispersed among the 'peoples'. These words bring vital affirmation: God was not rejecting or forgetting them, instead He described them as those with whom He was in 'covenant' (Zech. 9:11), 'like jewels in a crown' (v16) and 'attractive and beautiful' (v17).

8. Paul clearly states that 'All Scripture is God-breathed and is useful for teaching, rebuking, correcting and training in righteousness' (2 Tim. 3:16). Even difficult passages are to be read by everyone (not just learned theologians) because when we are open to God's Spirit, He reveals His truth – especially regarding His future plans and bigger picture.

Week Six: Broken staffs

Opening Icebreaker
The term 'shepherding' implies a close oversight, an attitude of care and self-sacrifice for the person or people to whom this is being provided. Sadly, politicians, in contrast, can have a reputation for self-seeking and self-promotion at the expense of others.

Aim of the Session
To understand the significance of God as the shepherd of our lives.

Discussion Starters

1. Wailing, crying or howling points to something giving cause for considerable grief, sorrow and trouble. The repeated use of this term suggests particular oppression being experienced. The ferocity of the subsequent Roman invasion suffered by the Jews (in AD 70) would be the reason for this degree of response. The use of the term 'cedar' (Zech. 11:2) points to the nation of Israel (see Jer. 22:6–7).

2. The accounts relating to God's people in the Old Testament consistently showed them as being in need of God's care, direction, provision and protection. Like sheep they were vulnerable and defenseless with strong tendencies to wander and get into trouble. The psalmist applied these terms of 'flock' and 'sheep' in that context (Psa. 78:52; 100:3; 119:176).

3. They were all shepherding actual sheep before God appointed them as leaders. As shepherds they therefore had insight as to what good leadership (of the Israelites) would entail (see 2 Sam. 7:7–8; Psa. 77:20; 78:70–72).

4. The use of these phrases confirmed that what Zechariah was saying and enacting was from God and not originating from himself. It showed that God was fully aware of the attitude and reaction of His people.

5. The actions of the 'foolish shepherd' (Zech. 11:15) in not only neglecting to provide proper and appropriate leadership but acting in a destructive manner, revealed his totally antagonistic and evil attitude towards God's people. Some consider this image as pointing to the antichrist. The subsequent verse describes God's judgment: 'May his arm be completely withered, his right eye totally blinded' (Zech. 11:17), indicative of this evil 'shepherd' having his power broken (which is specifically prophesied regarding the antichrist).

6. The Jewish religious leaders answered Pilate: 'We have no king but Caesar' (John 19:15). This decision to reject Jesus and instead have a Roman emperor to rule over them eventually resulted in the Roman army obliterating the nation and destroying Jerusalem under Titus in AD 70, following a rebellion by the Jews.

7. The law of Moses put the price of a slave as being worth 30 pieces of silver (Exod. 21:32). It added to the picture of Jesus being seen by the Jews to be someone with little value, and also reflected Isaiah's prophecy: 'He was despised and rejected by mankind, a man of suffering and familiar with pain. Like one from whom people hide their faces he was despised, and we held him in low esteem' (Isa. 53:3).

8. God wanted His people to respond, submit and follow Him as their mighty, caring and shepherd-like leader.

Week Seven: Beyond the horizon

Opening Icebreaker
The obvious modern technologies that would not have existed 60 years ago would include smartphones, tablets, laptops, satellite navigation systems and contactless debit cards. Science fiction has probably not predicted the speed and widespread use of such devices – smartphones only being commonly available since 2007.

Aim of the Session
To help us realise that God wants us to be aware of His plans for the future, which we are unable to envisage.

Discussion Starters

1. The phrase 'On that day' is used to preface God's powerful intervention to protect His people (Zech. 12:3,4,8), afflict His people's enemies (12:3,4,9; 14:13), empower His people against their attackers (12:6,8), bring spiritual revival and cleansing (12:11; 13:1,2,4; 14:20,21) and reveal His power (14:4,6,8,9).

2. Zechariah wanted to set the scene with great emphasis in respect of what was to follow in his prophecy (chapters 12–14). These were words from 'the LORD' who was all-powerful and able to fulfil exactly what He said; His word being wholly true and foretelling what was going to take place.

3. The details in Zechariah 12 show that God is fully aware of all schemes that will be planned against His people, and that He is fully in control of every situation, able to save them from seemingly inevitable physical annihilation.

4. Verses showing God's protection over His people when they are attacked include Zechariah 12:2–5,8–9; 14:3–5,10–15. These verses are a reminder that we can depend upon God's protection, especially in the spiritual realm, whatever may confront us (Psa. 46). In the context of this particular prophecy, there is a strong indication that this protection is a physical one relating to the Jews by God.

5. It's important to understand that both the Old and New Testaments (particularly the prophecies of Daniel, Ezekiel and Zechariah, and John in Revelation) are consistent in describing world events leading up to the return of Jesus in power and glory. The lack of a specific date of Jesus' return means we need to be in a state of ongoing preparation and continued dependence upon Him in the light of deteriorating spiritual, social and moral standards around us.

6. Jesus' words, 'Therefore keep watch' (Matt. 24:42), constitute a particular warning because Jesus will return 'at an hour when you do not expect him' (Matt. 24:44). This is a striking statement in view of the events leading up to His coming. They reinforce the need for each of us to see God's bigger picture in all that is taking place in contemporary political and social life.

7. These further details regarding the manner of Jesus' return point to the fact that His return will be totally unmistakable and that His identity will be wholly recognisable. Connected with His return is the fact that He will be accompanied by angels (Zech. 14:5b; Matt. 24:31; Rev. 19:13–14).

8. Peter describes cataclysmic events surrounding Christ's return (2 Pet. 3:10,12) similar to Zechariah's description (Zech. 14:7), and the need to be preparing, in spiritual terms, for that day (2 Pet. 3:11–12; Zech. 13:1–2).

Notes...

Notes...

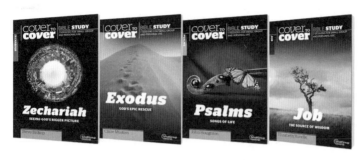

The *Cover to Cover* Bible Study Series

1 Corinthians
Growing a Spirit-filled church
ISBN: 978-1-85345-374-8

2 Corinthians
Restoring harmony
ISBN: 978-1-85345-551-3

1,2,3 John
Walking in the truth
ISBN: 978-1-78259-763-6

1 Peter
Good reasons for hope
ISBN: 978-1-78259-088-0

2 Peter
Living in the light of God's promises
ISBN: 978-1-78259-403-1

23rd Psalm
The Lord is my shepherd
ISBN: 978-1-85345-449-3

1 Timothy
Healthy churches – effective Christians
ISBN: 978-1-85345-291-8

2 Timothy and Titus
Vital Christianity
ISBN: 978-1-85345-338-0

Abraham
Adventures of faith
ISBN: 978-1-78259-089-7

Acts 1-12
Church on the move
ISBN: 978-1-85345-574-2

Acts 13-28
To the ends of the earth
ISBN: 978-1-85345-592-6

Barnabas
Son of encouragement
ISBN: 978-1-85345-911-5

Bible Genres
Hearing what the Bible really says
ISBN: 978-1-85345-987-0

Daniel
Living boldly for God
ISBN: 978-1-85345-986-3

David
A man after God's own heart
ISBN: 978-1-78259-444-4

Ecclesiastes
Hard questions and spiritual answers
ISBN: 978-1-85345-371-7

Elijah
A man and his God
ISBN: 978-1-85345-575-9

Elisha
A lesson in faithfulness
ISBN: 978-1-78259-494-9

Ephesians
Claiming your inheritance
ISBN: 978-1-85345-229-1

Esther
For such a time as this
ISBN: 978-1-85345-511-7

Exodus
God's epic rescue
ISBN: 978-1-78951-272-4

Ezekiel
A prophet for all times
ISBN: 978-1-78259-836-7

Fruit of the Spirit
Growing more like Jesus
ISBN: 978-1-85345-375-5

Galatians
Freedom in Christ
ISBN: 978-1-85345-648-0

Genesis 1-11
Foundations of reality
ISBN: 978-1-85345-404-2

Genesis 12-50
Founding fathers of faith
ISBN: 978-1-78259-960-9

God's Rescue Plan
Finding God's fingerprints on human history
ISBN: 978-1-85345-294-9

Great Prayers of the Bible
Applying them to our lives today
ISBN: 978-1-85345-253-6

Habakkuk
Choosing God's way
ISBN: 978-1-78259-843-5

Haggai
Motivating God's people
ISBN: 978-1-78259-686-8

Hebrews
Jesus – simply the best
ISBN: 978-1-85345-337-3

Isaiah 1-39
Prophet to the nations
ISBN: 978-1-85345-510-0

Isaiah 40-66
Prophet of restoration
ISBN: 978-1-85345-550-6

Jacob
Taking hold of God's blessing
ISBN: 978-1-78259-685-1

James
Faith in action
ISBN: 978-1-85345-293-2

Jeremiah
The passionate prophet
ISBN: 978-1-85345-372-4

Job
The source of wisdom
ISBN: 978-1-78259-992-0

Joel
Getting real with God
ISBN: 978-1-78951-927-2

John's Gospel
Exploring the seven miraculous signs
ISBN: 978-1-85345-295-6

Jonah
Rescued from the depths
ISBN: 978-1-78259-762-9

Joseph
The power of forgiveness and reconciliation
ISBN: 978-1-85345-252-9

Joshua 1-10
Hand in hand with God
ISBN: 978-1-85345-542-7

Joshua 11-24
Called to service
ISBN: 978-1-78951-138-3

Judges 1-8
The spiral of faith
ISBN: 978-1-85345-681-7

Judges 9-21
Learning to live God's way
ISBN: 978-1-85345-910-8

Luke
A prescription for living
ISBN: 978-1-78259-270-9

Mark
Life as it is meant to be lived
ISBN: 978-1-85345-233-8

Mary
The mother of Jesus
ISBN: 978-1-78259-402-4

Moses
Face to face with God
ISBN: 978-1-85345-336-6

Names of God
Exploring the depths of God's character
ISBN: 978-1-85345-680-0

Nehemiah
Principles for life
ISBN: 978-1-85345-335-9

Parables
Communicating God on earth
ISBN: 978-1-85345-340-3

Philemon
From slavery to freedom
ISBN: 978-1-85345-453-0

Philippians
Living for the sake of the gospel
ISBN: 978-1-85345-421-9

Prayers of Jesus
Hearing His heartbeat
ISBN: 978-1-85345-647-3

Proverbs
Living a life of wisdom
ISBN: 978-1-85345-373-1

Psalms
Songs of life
ISBN: 978-1-78951-240-3

Revelation 1-3
Christ's call to the Church
ISBN: 978-1-85345-461-5

Revelation 4-22
The Lamb wins! Christ's final victory
ISBN: 978-1-85345-411-0

Rivers of Justice
Responding to God's call to righteousness today
ISBN: 978-1-85345-339-7

Ruth
Loving kindness in action
ISBN: 978-1-85345-231-4

Song of Songs
A celebration of love
ISBN: 978-1-78259-959-3

The Armour of God
Living in His strength
ISBN: 978-1-78259-583-0

The Beatitudes
Immersed in the grace of Christ
ISBN: 978-1-78259-495-6

The Creed
Belief in action
ISBN: 978-1-78259-202-0

The Divine Blueprint
God's extraordinary power in ordinary lives
ISBN: 978-1-85345-292-5

The Holy Spirit
Understanding and experiencing Him
ISBN: 978-1-85345-254-3

The Image of God
His attributes and character
ISBN: 978-1-85345-228-4

The Kingdom
Studies from Matthew's Gospel
ISBN: 978-1-85345-251-2

The Letter to the Colossians
In Christ alone
ISBN: 978-1-855345-405-9

The Letter to the Romans
Good news for everyone
ISBN: 978-1-85345-250-5

The Lord's Prayer
Praying Jesus' way
ISBN: 978-1-85345-460-8

The Prodigal Son
Amazing grace
ISBN: 978-1-85345-412-7

The Second Coming
Living in the light of Jesus' return
ISBN: 978-1-85345-422-6

The Sermon on the Mount
Life within the new covenant
ISBN: 978-1-85345-370-0

Thessalonians
Building Church in changing times
ISBN: 978-1-78259-443-7

The Ten Commandments
Living God's way
ISBN: 978-1-85345-593-3

The Uniqueness of our Faith
What makes Christianity distinctive?
ISBN: 978-1-85345-232-1

Zechariah
Seeing God's bigger picture
ISBN: 978-1-78951-263-2

Be inspired by God.
Every day.

Confidently face life's challenges by equipping yourself daily with God's Word. There is something for everyone...

Every Day with Jesus

Selwyn Hughes' renowned writing is updated by Mick Brooks into these trusted and popular notes.

Life Every Day

Jeff Lucas helps apply the Bible to daily life with his trademark humour and insight.

Inspiring Women
Every Day

Encouragement, uplifting scriptures and insightful daily thoughts for women.

The Manual

Straight-talking guides to help men walk daily with God. Written by Carl Beech.

To find out more about all our daily Bible reading notes, or to take out a subscription, visit **cwr.org.uk/biblenotes** or call 01252 784700.
Also available in Christian bookshops.

 Printed format   Large print format   Email format   Ebook format